THE SPRINGS

THE desert communities that collectively make up the Palm Springs area are Palm Springs, Desert Hot Springs, Cathedral City, Rancho Mirage, Palm Desert, Indian Wells, La Quinta, Indio and Coachella. They are strung like precious green emeralds along the 26 miles of the Coachella Valley east of Los Angeles. An oasis in the desert, the valley is held safely between the arms of the Santa Rosa and Little San Bernadino mountain ranges. Protected from the pollution, noise and congestion of the west coast by a mountain pass, yet easily accessible, Palm Springs is just a two hour drive from Los Angeles.

Centuries ago, a branch of the Cahuilla Indians discovered the "magical and sacred" waters of the hot springs on the valley floor. When Spanish explorers happened upon the valley in 1774 they dubbed the Indians Agua Caliente, translated as hot water, and by the 1800's the site had become a stagecoach stop and one-store railroad town.

Today, the area has evolved into "America's foremost desert resort." The lush green valley flows gracefully into the incredibly and wildly beautiful mountains and high desert country surrounding it. The year-round wonderful weather with warm days and cool nights has attracted many of Hollywood's greatest stars to make their homes here.

The growing number of resorts, hotels, inns, shopping malls, golf courses and recreation opportunities, as well as fine and performing arts facilities, has drawn ever-increasing numbers of visitors. More than two million people visit the area each year, playing golf and tennis, camping, hiking, horseback riding, cross-country skiing on Mt. Jan Jacinto or just soaking up the warm desert sun around one of the more than 8,000 swimming pools in the valley.

More than a thousand years ago, the Agua Caliente Indians discovered the soothing mineral properties of the hot springs in the Coachella Valley. White men took considerably longer to make their own discoveries.

In 1853, railroad surveyors first sampled the waters. Stage coach passengers in the 1860's spread the word and in 1884 John Guthrie McCallum became the valley's first permanent white settler and founder of Palm Springs.

It wasn't until 1886 when Dr. Welwood Murray, a canny Scotsman with an eye to the

future, built the Palm Springs Hotel as a haven for people with respiratory illnesses, that the area's future was cast. Soon, "The Springs," so close to Los Angeles, became a favorite hideaway for Hollywood stars.

In 1936, film stars Ralph Bellamy and Charlie Farrell, tired of waiting for a tennis court, bought some desert land and built their own. The Racquet Club attracted such luminaries as Clark Gable, Humphrey Bogart and Henry Fonda as Palm Springs' fame spread. Pictured above is an early scene along Palm Canyon Drive. The changes are apparent in the photo on the following page.

5

PALM Canyon Drive, Palm Springs' main thoroughfare, is not only the city's main arterial street but its main shopping street as well. What began as a dusty two-way dirt road has evolved into a one-way three-lane, five-mile thoroughfare lined with more than 1800 palm trees. Each long, lingering dusk, the trees serve as illuminated street lights, leading the way toward the dusky pink and shadowy blue bulk of the sheer San Jacinto Mountains.

Shopping along Palm Canyon Drive is as pleasant as the valley itself. Strolling the sidewalks or enjoying a leisurely ride in one of the horse-drawn carriages is a favorite activity of residents and visitors alike. The shops feature

everything from furs, jewelry, clothing, home furnishings and crafts to tempt any fancy.

In addition to shopping, the drive offers an impressive array of fascinating art galleries and restaurants.

For a bit of Palm Springs history, visit the McCallum Adobe at the Village Green at the South end of Palm Canyon Drive. Each brick surrounding the fountain contains the names of individuals and families who donated to help create this beautiful setting.

Palm Canyon Drive offers an atmosphere of promenade both day and evening, although luxury cars including chauffeur-driven limousines, Bentleys and Mercedes often outnumber pedestrians. Many of the finest stores in the world have branches on Palm Canyon Drive, which has been likened to Rodeo Drive in Beverly Hills, but here, shop-

ping is done casual style. The warm sunny days make leisurely shopping expeditions a joy.

The Desert Inn Fashion Plaza and the Palm Springs Mall are both air-conditioned enclosed complete shopping centers designed to meet the needs and interests of locals and visitors alike.

After a day of browsing and shopping on Palm Canyon Drive, the perfect activity is to relax in the hot mineral pools. No matter how good your health, these soothing "magic" waters unkink muscles and leave you feeling wonderfully alive and well.

The Indians' wisdom in picking this valley for their home is still evident today. The San Jacinto Mountains cascade to within blocks of Palm Canyon Drive, providing a ruggedly beautiful backdrop to one of the finest shopping arcades anywhere. To the west, the mountains form a barrier against the grey haze which blankets the California coast. The warm dry climate, with average daytime temperatures of 88 and cool nights averaging 55, beckons outdoor enthusiasts to enjoy a wide array of sports activities, including a round of golf at one of the over 80 golf courses in the area.

Paying tribute to Palm Springs' founding, on opposite page, a recreation of the Byzantine-Moorish tower which graced the old El Mirador Hotel stands as part of the Desert Hospital complex, built on the site of the 1927 hotel.

FROM the first health spa for Native Americans to the playground of the stars, Palm Springs, an oasis amidst miles of sand and cactus, comes alive each morning as the sun sends its warming rays across the beautiful Coachella Valley.

T HE airport fountain, with its cascading waters, set against the steep San Jacinto range, is the first inspiring site air travelers to Palm Springs Regional Airport see. Handsome Mount San Jacinto, with its snow topped 10,831 ft. crest, provides a striking contrast to the brown hills, stark desert and carefully manicured green golf courses, such as those pictured here, which spread like velvety carpeting across the floor of the Coachella Valley.

Although Palm Springs attracts most of its visitors with vacationing in mind, many find

that doing business here is almost as plea-
surable as enjoying a round of golf or a dip
in the pool. The state-of-the-art Palm Springs
Convention Center, at right, provides the
finest in meeting facilities and exhibition
spaces for those who travel to this desert
oasis on business.

Less than two hours from Los Angeles' smog and crowds, the Coachella Valley has become a resort mecca for a wide variety of souls including the very wealthy, the rich-and-famous, weary business people and families seeking the warm, relaxed lifestyle so well represented by this desert valley.

There are 26 miles of vibrant towns and lush resorts within the protected confines of the valley. Exploring and sampling the more than 80 golf courses and dozens of country clubs is a labor of love for any visitor. Teeing up on a cool, dry desert morning on a lush green fairway with a snow-capped mountain over your shoulder is a not to be missed experience.

Each of the nine towns in the valley has a flavor unique unto itself and invites exploration day and evening. As the sun goes down over these clean, uncluttered cities, bringing with it cool breezes, evening offers its own special attractions under a sky almost impossibly clear and starlit.

First known as a health spa area, then a tennis mecca, Palm Springs has become the "Golf Capital of the World." Currently the Coachella Valley is home to 80 golf courses ranging from nine-hole executive to 18-hole championship courses. Four of those courses have been rated among the top 100 in the nation by Golf Digest magazine. The Dinah Shore Mission Hills Country Club course ranks among the top 20 in California as well.

Each year, the Coachella Valley and Palm Springs is host to many major golf events

including such well known tournaments as the Nabisco Dinah Shore, the Bob Hope Chrysler Classic and The Skins Game. These tournaments are hosted at such highly rated courses as PGA West, Big Horn and Mission Hills, to name a few. The superb quality of these courses draws the world's best golfers as well as being favorites of political figures and television and movie celebrities. Pictured here are just a few of the sun drenched courses the valley offers: Cathedral Canyon Country Club, lower left; Mission Hills Golf Course, above, and the Desert Princess Golf Course. Also pictured is Dinah Shore at the Nabisco Classic.

WHETHER drawn to this green and golden paradise for business or pleasure, Palm Springs and the Coachella Valley goes a long way toward providing a truly unique experience. The valley offers a plethora of luxury resorts like the Palm Springs Riviera Hotel, at right, with its new pool-side suites.

Each of the valley's spectacular resorts has its

own special ambience and style. Marriott's Rancho Las Palmas Resort and Country Club in Rancho Mirage, pictured above left, has been newly refurbished. Stouffers Esmeralda Resort, above, sprawls enticingly at the foot of the San Jacinto Mountains. La Quinta Hotel Golf and Tennis Resort, far left, has been rated one of the top 50 tennis resorts in the country by Tennis magazine.

The cool white marble Palm Springs Hilton Resort and Racquet Club, above, is an elegant plant-filled retreat. The Palm Springs Marquis, at left, is a posh desert-modern edifice with gourmet eating and extensive meeting and convention facilities as well as pools, tennis and spa. The large and lovely Wyndham Hotel, top of page, offers yet another brand of luxury accommodations on the valley floor.

The Hyatt Grand Champions, pictured at top right, plays host to the top ranked men and womens' tennis tournaments in their multi- million dollar state of the art tennis stadium.

The Westin Mission Hills Resort in Rancho Mirage, pictured at the top of this page, has recently reopened after a year-long $70 million renovation. The hotel now has not one but two 18-hole emerald green golf courses, one of which was designed by golf pro Gary Player.

The Ritz Carlton, above, sits high atop the hills overlooking the city of Rancho Mirage. Guests can play tennis to their heart's content on one of 10 courts or lounge poolside while watching wild bighorn sheep nibbling the grass almost within touching distance.

The nearly new Doubletree Resort at Desert Princess has a marvelous 18-hole championship golf course, tennis and racquetball courts, pools, spas and a health club.

Although it is most commonly known as the "Golf Capital of the World," the Palm Springs area earned its first celebrity status when Ralph Bellamy and Charlie Farrell built their tennis resort in

1936. Today, four of Tennis magazine's top 50 tennis resorts are in the valley. Among them is Marriott's Desert Springs Resort in Palm Desert, pictured on this page.

This premier resort complex offers the finest in accommodations, the most luxurious spa facilities in the desert and two challenging 18-hole golf courses. The entire complex is threaded with a series of waterways complete with boats to transport guests around the resort.

FERRELL and Bellamy really started something with their Racquet Club. With the help of a little public relations, Palm Springs soon became the" Playground of the Stars." Today, the valley is home to over 700 millionaires, many of them Hollywood movie and television stars. It is not uncommon, while attending a fund raiser or theater performance, to rub elbows with the likes of Dinah Shore, former president Gerald Ford or Bette Midler. Palm Springs' previous mayor was Sonny Bono.

It is considered high honor to have a street named after you and Bob Hope and Frank Sinatra are among those so honored. Both have homes in the valley. Hope's 'humble abode' built on a ridge overlooking the valley in Southridge, pictured at right, has been likened to an airline terminal in size. It's not quite that large but would certainly house a substantial department store and is easily seen from the desert floor.

Frank Sinatra's home, lacking nothing in splendor and luxury, lower right, is in nearby Rancho Mirage.

Stars whose names shall live in history, such as Mary Martin, Liberace and Elvis Presley have also lived here. Pictured below is one of

Elvis Presley's Palm Springs homes. At right, second from top, is the home of flamboyant pianist Liberace.

Walter Annenberg, financier and former media mogul, has an estate, pictured far left, in Rancho Mirage on the corners of Bob Hope and Frank Sinatra Drives. The story goes that he was denied membership in a local golf club so he built his own course. The Annenberg Estate is often referred to as the retreat of presidents. Every president since Herbert Hoover, with the exception of Jimmy Carter, has visited Rancho Mirage.

THE Palm Springs area isn't just the playground of the stars. Exclusive El Paseo caters to the rich and elite, for shopping on an international scale. 360 days of sunshine draws visitors to enjoy the warm, dry climate. Horseback riding, playing a round of golf on the same courses played and designed by such greats as Arnold Palmer or smashing a tennis ball around courts frequented by Ivan Lendl are just a few of the enticements. As outside temperatures climb, you can even throw some ice slivers behind your skates at the Ice Capades Chalet located in the

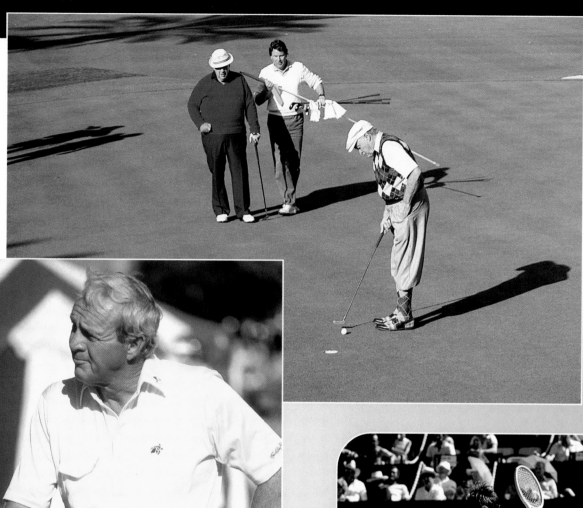

elaborate Palm Desert Town Center. This large shopping mall offers the finest in shopping from exclusive boutiques to major retailers.

The Desert Museum, lower left, an $8.5 million arts center, features a western arts wing, a natural science wing and the Annenberg Theater.

Polo, one of the world's oldest team sports, is well represented at the valley's two polo clubs and attracts many world-famous players, including Britain's Prince Charles. Eldorado Polo Club is open November to April and the Empire Polo Club year-round.

ACH day, visitors board one of two 80-passenger cable cars for the 15-minute ascent from the desert floor of the rugged Chino Canyon on the north edge of Palm Springs to the 8,516 foot Mountain Station. The summit of Mount San Jacinto requires an additional hike to the 10,831 foot crest. The cable cars traverse one of the sheerest mountains in North America, sliding over granite recesses deeper than the Grand Canyon, going through five climatic zones in the process and are suspended from towers hundreds of feet tall perched on ledges along the craggy mountain.

The Palm Springs Aerial Tramway is the world's largest single-span, double-reversible lift. At the top of the lift, visitors are deposited

in a pine-scented alpine-type forest, 40 degrees cooler than the desert floor they left so far below. This is the doorway to Mount San Jacinto State Park and Wilderness, a wonderland of hiking and equestrian trails, campgrounds and breath-taking views of Palm Springs and hundreds of miles of desert and valley beyond.

Built in the 1960's by a Swiss company, the tramway has been referred to as the "eighth engineering wonder of the world." Over a two year period, 20,000 helicopter missions were flown to haul men and materials onto the narrow ledges of the mountain to construct the support towers for the tram.

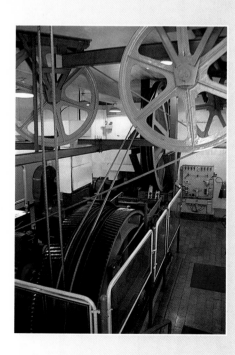

I N the days when the Agua Caliente Indians roamed the desert, they sought summer refuge from the blistering heat within the sheltering canyons of the Coachella Valley. These canyons, which divide the San Jacinto Mountains from the Santa Rosas, were oasis of cool, shady palm stands, waterfalls and handsome gorges. Today, these canyons, including Palm, Andreas, and Murray Canyons, are known as the Indian Canyons and are still owned by the Agua Caliente Indians. Visitors to the canyons, five miles from downtown Palm Springs, can enjoy the grove of more than 3,000 palm trees in Palm Canyon, horse-

back ride, picnic and hike amid the towering rock faces and mysterious caves and crevices that make up the canyons. Back in the recesses of the canyons, explorers still find pottery shards, ruins of dwellings atop the cliff walls and petroglyph or picture rocks - mute testimony to generations of Native Americans past.

The valley narrows as you travel south into the Indian Canyons, squeezing through a slot in the rock called Split Rock, above.

From there, the road climbs to Hermit's Bench where a gift shop marks the beginning of your adventure into Indian Canyons.

More than 1,200 acres of native desert has been set aside as a living monument to desert wildlife and a botanical park. The Living Desert in Palm Desert is the west's most complete introduction to the natural world of the desert. Represented are the flora and fauna of eight different desert habitats as well as a home for some of the world's most endangered species like the Grevy's zebra, the aardwolf and the Arabian Oryx, the unicorn of the desert.

The Living Desert is a refuge for bighorn or Rocky Mountain sheep. These swift, agile and tireless creatures, once common throughout much of western North America, have become increasingly rare, hunted indiscriminately almost to extinction. This sturdy animal grows to about 40 inches in height and weighs as much as 300 pounds. The males

have large curving horns which can measure as long as 42 inches around the curve. In the spring they can be seen exerting their dominance against other males by crashing their horns violently together.

Another resident of the Living Desert is the amusing roadrunner. This silly bird got his name from his habit of racing along the road at speeds clocked at up to 15 miles per hour. When this rather large bird, as much as two feet long including his one foot tail, wants to stop, he turns aside and brakes to a quick halt by throwing his long tail over his head. A helpful bird, the roadrunner's diet staple is snakes, including the poisonous varieties.

The increasingly uncommon barn owl also makes his home here. Strictly nocturnal, this large, light-colored bird with the heart-shaped face and silent flight, is not often seen by visitors in other parts of the desert. Its diet, again a help to mankind, consists mainly of rodents.

Many think of the desert as an arid wasteland of blowing sand and blistering heat. The desert of the Coachella Valley, thanks to its elevations and irrigation from the Colorado River Basin is, instead, a mecca of agricultural wealth. Agriculture vies with tourism as the valley's main industry.

Begun in the late 1800's with vegetables and cattle, crops branched out in the 1920's to include citrus, table grapes and dates. Crops are grown and harvested year-round. The date harvest begins in late fall and is finished in December.

In the eastern portion of the valley thousands of acres of stately date palms thrive. This area grows nearly 98% of the Western Hemisphere's supply of dates. Roadside stands feature date shakes, practically the valley's signature drink. Also available are date cakes, cookies, pudding and date sugar.

The date clusters hang high on these towering palm trees. Pickers ride moving platforms, hang from harnesses, climb 40-foot ladders or ride mechanical booms to harvest the 20 to 30 pound clusters of 200 or so lusciously sweet fruits.

The city of Indio, the "Date Capital of the World," where the first date orchards in the valley were established, has held an annual National Date Festival every year since 1921. The event, at the Desert ExpoCentre, is staged each February and includes such attractions as an Arabian Nights Pageant, a carnival and ostrich and camel races.

THE Mojave (pronounced mo-hav-ee) or High Desert as it is called, the northernmost desert in California, begins just over the mountain range north of Los Angeles and sweeps eastward to the Colorado River.

Called "a great and mysterious wasteland" by author John Steinbeck this area is called "High Desert" because of its elevation of 3,000 to more than 6,000 feet above sea level. Here, broad sandy sweeps alternate with bleached salt flats glistening like diamonds in the sun and rough mountain terrain, tortured and blasted by wind and blowing sand to create sculpture unique to nature. It is a land of rich contrasts with piles of granite boulders often reaching heights of 100 feet scattered across arid desert sands, creating a stark and awesome beauty. Yet, in spring, the desert transforms itself

into a garden of softly hued flowering plants for a short span of time in an age-old rite of renewal.

Joshua Tree National Monument, east of Palm Springs, is a half-million acre preserve named for one of the oddest of the desert's plants. Actually a member of the lily family, the Joshua tree grows from 20 to 40 feet in height, sending its roots deep into the sand in search of water. It is believed that the Mormons named the tree for Joshua, raising his arms to lead his children into the promised land. The Indians found a less noble purpose for the trees, making shampoo and laxatives from it and using the fibers for hunting nets and sandals. They also roasted the heavenly waxy greenish-white blooms and served them as a delicacy. Some of the trees are estimated to be more than 300 years old and serve, as always, as havens for wildlife.

Many types of cacti also thrive in the dry desert, including the spiny ocotillo, far left. The cholla, above, leaves a free souvenir with anyone unlucky enough to brush against it. If touched, an entire limb dislodges from the plant and sticks firmly, and painfully, to its new host.

Each spring, if it's not too dry and the desert is blessed with its usual meager five inches of rain, an amazing change comes over the land. The normally ungainly, thick, spiky cacti of the desert, as if to compensate for their unlovely appearance, come alive with large, showy, fragrant blossoms. Suddenly the desert is alive with color and scent for a few short weeks.

Despite the desert's reputation of being inhospitable, the area supports a wide variety of wild and plant life, all adapted to the special living condition of the region. The tiny kangaroo rat with its tufted tail shares space with coyotes and jackrabbit as well as 38 species of lizards, reptiles and amphibians and 249 varieties of birds. The many varieties of cacti have thick, strong skins with bristly spikes to protect their soft inner cores which are designed to store water throughout the long desert droughts.

Truly one of the last frontiers in America, the desert remains largely unspoiled, unsettled and untamed by man. Here the overwhelming natural beauty of waves of rolling sands, black cinder cones thrusting from the desert floor and miles of muted browns and dusty greens of the desert flora are free, each spring, to suddenly erupt in bloom. Riotous sheets of orange and yellow California poppies carpet the valleys, their color so bright it can be seen for more than 10 miles.

The distinctive spiny ocotillo produces brilliant orange/red blossoms while the hedgehog or echinocereus cactus, left, produces huge, fragrant flowers, one to a stem. Flat-stemmed prickly pear cactus produce yellow or reddish flowers, followed by a pear-shaped fruit that is not only good to eat but a valuable source of water in the moisture-starved desert.

Mesquite, creosote, yellow coreopsis, desert candles, heliotrope and verbena all combine to create a sea of rainbow colors on the desert floor each March, climbing to the higher elevations through the month of June, and then returning to the soft greens and browns of the resting desert, awaiting yet another spring and the promise of renewal.

THE Coachella Valley is truly a vacationer's paradise. The clean, uncluttered cities with their fashionable and varied shopping, fine dining, wonderful art galleries and plentiful theater and musical establishments are beyond compare. The spas, resorts, and hotels offer a choice of luxury accommodations in any budget category and to rival any in the world. There are over 80 lush green golf courses to challenge the duffer, dozens of tennis facilities, horseback riding, hiking, cross-country skiing a mountaintop or more than 8,000 swimming pools to lounge around, soaking up the 360 days of sunshine. There's rubbing elbows with the elite of the movie and television world, galas, festivals, a breathtaking tramway ride. There's stark and lovely scenery, a glimpse into the life of desert wildlife and glimpses into the ancient past of the Native Americans who first settled here. There are the Indian Canyons, the desert in bloom, bighorn sheep grazing almost within touching distance, dramatic snow-frosted mountains and whimsical Joshua trees. All these things greet you in the Coachella Valley but, there's more...for those who have spent the night in revelry or those who would rise in the cool, chill predawn hours there's a very special time...

In the Desert night, under a canopy of stars that seems endless and eternal, it is time for owls to hunt on silent wings amidst the strange and eerie shapes of cacti and Joshua trees. With the coming of dawn, haunting silhouettes of cacti dissolve slowly and the desert awakens in glorious shades of pink, amber, gold, crimson and vermillion. Gliding into the clear desert sky, the sun reflects off the sand crystals, making them glisten like a multitude of diamonds.

Slowly, the colors of the desert change, dusty black to raw sienna, depthless grey to burnt umber, yellow ocher, dun and muted green under a sky shading to ultramarine and Prussian blue. These are moments unique to the desert, to be cherished by those privileged to experience them, to be stored in the soul forever, to nourish us in times not so golden and pure.